THE BOY INSIDE THE MAN
Copyright © 2022 by Donovan Gardner

Paperback ISBN: 9798447741921

Cover design by Ashley J. Gardner.

Published by Gardner Books.

The Boy Inside the Man

A memoir of childhood trauma

Gardner Books
2022

1

MY MOTHER HAD me in Allendale, South Carolina at the age of sixteen. I was a product of her and my father's rocky high school relationship. I see now that they both had struggles that they were dealing with that would affect their parenting of me (or lack thereof) on into adulthood. My mother left me in the care of her mother, "Granny," and went on to finish high school, and then attend a nursing school in Brooklyn.

Granny raised me with a lot of love and a lot of church. She attended the local African Methodist Episcopal (AME) church in town. The quiet services saying prayers and singing hymnals were something that I loved, especially since it was a chance to spend time with my Granny. And it ended up giving me the foundational relationship with God that would help carry me through the devastating times to come in later years. When we were at home, Granny loved to share stories with me about what things were like when she was growing up. And I loved hearing them. This was my life for my early childhood. My father provided money to help me with things I needed like school supplies and clothes. Most weekends he would come by Granny's house and we'd stand out on the porch and talk for a few minutes before he left. It was a stiff, awkward exchange. More like two new neighbors introducing one another than a father speaking with the son he hasn't seen in a week. Mama came home to visit when she got breaks at school. Those were my favorite times. Mom and I were like two peas in a pod. She was my confidant, my playmate, my best friend in the world, even though I didn't get to see her as often as I'd like.

As far as I knew, this was a normal, happy life. But it wouldn't last long.

On Christmas Eve of 1993, I was six years old. I couldn't always get everything

I wanted on Christmas, but I got enough to satisfy my little heart and create a joyous holiday for Granny and me. But the greatest gift I received was always the visit from my mother as she got her breaks from school. The excitement of being off from school, getting toys, and getting to see Mama was overwhelming. This was the happiest time of the year for me.

When my mother arrived, I was just as happy to see her as ever. I heard the taxi she usually hired pull up into our driveway and I beelined to the front door, Granny telling me to stop running before I fell and hurt myself. I speed-walked the rest of the way and opened the door to find my mother standing in the driveway beside a large truck with "U-Haul" on the side. Not a cab. Then I realized she'd brought someone with her. A man. Who wasn't my father. I was surprised and confused. But then my mother explained and I was terrified.

She wanted me to go with her and her new boyfriend to live in Orlando. Granny was just as stunned as I was. Neither of us had gotten any direct warning, or even hints, that this was going to happen. I was comfortable where I was, comfortable living with her and attending church and playing with my friends at school. I didn't want to leave. But I did want to be with my mom. If I went with her, we could see each other all the time instead of every now and then. But I didn't know this guy, Dalton was his name. He seemed nice enough, but did that mean we needed to move to a different state with him? And what about Daddy? Would I ever be able to see him again?

In the end, Mama took me to Orlando with her. After all, even though Granny had spent all this time raising me, she was still my mother and I was her child, not Granny's. So she got me packed up with all my Christmas gifts and, just after Christmas Mama, Dalton, and I all piled into the U-Haul and set off for Orlando. I'd never seen my Granny look so sad. And as I watched her in the side mirror of the truck, I felt the same way. I cried silently between Dalton and Mama on the bench seat most of the way there.

The transition was tough. But I eventually started to settle in okay. Dalton was a steady, fatherly presence in the house that I appreciated, though it would have been nice to have my own father around. It wasn't long before my mother was pregnant. I was going to have a little brother! This was new for me because this child would be a boy like me. My father had a few other children, but they were all daughters. It was fascinating to watch my mother's stomach grow and know that my little brother was inside. She explained to me that this was how I was made, too. I was in awe. We even became close friends with another family who lived nearby. My mom had become best friends with Zaria Johnson and it wasn't long before they were like blood relatives to us. The Johnsons were a family of four with a wife, Zariah, husband, Carter, their daughter, Ruby, and Carter's brother, Joseph, who we kids called "Uncle Joe." At this point, my new living situation was starting to feel more and more like 'home.' I felt like I had people around me who I could trust who loved and cared about me. It was comfortable, stable, and safe, even if it was new.

One day when I was at school during this time, I was running through the hallway while there was some kind of professional cleaning going on. I tripped over a hose, careened out of the school doors, and crashed into a metal fence post outside. Head-first.

At that point, I passed out, my little body having experienced too much head trauma to stay awake and alert. The next thing

I knew, the darkness started to fade. I started to feel and hear sound again. Now, instead of the pitch black of a coma, I saw the deep red of the back of my eyelids, feeling sunlight on my face, a blanket over my body, and a bed of some kind beneath my back. I could hear someone praying fervently somewhere nearby.

When I opened my eyes, Mama, Granny, Dalton, Uncle Joe, Mrs. Johnson, and a nurse were all in the room. Granny was the one praying at my bedside, Mrs. Johnson was praying out the window, and Mama was being comforted by Dalton and Uncle Joe. The nurse was checking the machine beside me. Granny, Mrs. Johnson, and Mama looked grateful, Mama immediately rushing over to check me and hug me to her bulbous stomach. Ronnia and Uncle Joe looked relieved. The nurse looked stunned, as if she'd seen a ghost or watched someone rise from the dead. But she quickly slapped a smile on her face and started asking me questions about how I felt. She even got me a small cup of water to sip on since my throat felt like sandpaper.

I eventually learned what had happened. Hitting the pole had literally split my skull open. Mama was called and I was immediately rushed to the hospital. Uncle Joe drove Mrs. Johnson to the hospital and Granny came down as soon as she could. Mama apparently arrived just in time to watch the surgeon staple my scalp back onto my skull and she fainted at the sight of it. With her being about eight months pregnant, she was put in her own bed and monitored. At the time, the doctors weren't sure that I would ever wake up because the damage to my head was so extensive. And on the slim chance that I did wake up, there was little hope that I would be able to speak, walk, or do anything else like a healthy seven-year-old boy. From memory loss to paralysis they had no way of knowing how bad the damage would be on a long-term basis.

With me being out for days, and knowing that every hour I stayed in the coma decreased the chances that I would ever wake up at all, everyone was getting worried and tense about how this was going to turn out. Would I wake up? If I did, would I be like I was or somehow impaired like the doctors feared? When I woke up, recognized everyone, was able to speak, and could even move my arms and legs, there was plenty of praise to go around. Against all odds, I had made it, and we attributed that to faith.

And after a few months of staying home from school to heal—Granny and Uncle Joe taking turns watching over me when Mama and Dalton couldn't—I was completely back to normal. This had been my first experience believing that God had something to do with directly helping me. As far as I could tell, he had saved my young life.

2

BY AGE TEN, I had fully adjusted to my new life with my stepfather, Dalton, my 3-year-old brother, Patrick, and Mama. I still got to see Granny and would often spend weeks or months with her during the summer. That was an opportunity to reconnect with old friends and spend time with her. I got to visit the old AME church she went to, but now that I was a bit older, I struggled to stay awake and was itching to get out of there as quickly as possible when the service was over. Even thought I was still young, I loved God and appreciated all the blessings that I had. Yet something about those quiet, subdued services now began to bore me to tears. But it was still nice to be able to spend time with Granny.

Depending upon what kind of appointments or work schedule Mama and Dalton had, I would sometimes get dropped off at the Johnsons and Mr. Johnson would drive me and Ruby to school. On one of those occasions, Mama had gotten me and Patrick up extra early so that she could get to where she needed to be. She'd made arrangements with a sitter to stay with Patrick for the day at home. When I got to the Johnson's I plopped myself down on the couch in front of the television to watch cartoons. Ruby came in to grab a comb off one of the tables beside the couch and I waved to her as she scrambled back to her room to finish getting ready. Mr. Johnson walked by while pulling a shirt on, stopping just long enough to rub my head in greeting before continuing down the house's main hallway to the master bedroom to finish getting ready for work.

"Hey, D. Come here for a second," I heard, snapping me out of my focus on the goofy animals on the screen. I turned to find Uncle Joe at the opening of the hallway. I figured he must need help with something, so

I abandoned my show and walked over to him.

"Sir?"

"Come on in for a second, I wanna talk to you," he said, ushering me into his own room, which was right at the beginning of the hallway. I moved into it, looking around at the small, clean room and neatly-made bed. When my gaze circled back around to the door, he was shutting it and locking it, which I found strange. Apparently, whatever he wanted to talk about was a secret. I knew Ruby's birthday was next month, so this had to be about some kind of big gift or party. I tried to stay cool and calm. If I looked too excited he might think he couldn't trust me to not say anything to Ruby.

"Sit, sit," he said, taking a seat on the end of the bed and patting the space beside him. So I sat. He was taking a lot of time to build up to this secret, so I figured it had to be a pretty big one. Maybe a PlayStation? That would be an expensive gift, but Ruby and I didn't play video games much. I tried to focus on what Uncle Joe was going to say since he obviously knew what he wanted to get for his niece. There was no point in speculating if he was going to tell me anyway.

"First, how's school going?" he asked.

"Okay. English is kinda hard, but it's okay. I think I like math the most right now. Mrs. Anderson always tells funny stories."

He smiled. "That's good. Liking your teachers helps you learn. How's Sissy and Lil' Man doing?"

These were the nicknames that my Uncle Joe had made up for my mother and Patrick.

"Good. Patrick poops a lot, but Mama's cool."

"That's good. That's real good," Uncle Joe said. Just as I was wondering what this all has to do with what he wanted to get Ruby for her birthday, Uncle Joe put his hand on my knee.

I jerked my knee away. This made him hesitate for only a moment before he grabbed between my legs. When I tried to stand to get away from him, he grabbed a fistful of my shirt, drawing me toward him as he clapped a hand over my mouth before I could cry out. I swung my fists, but they hit his chest and stomach and he didn't seem to feel them. I beat at his wrist and forearm, but I might as well have been fighting against a tree branch. My ten-year-old body didn't stand a chance against a fully grown man.

He pushed me down on the bed, telling me "This is your fault," and "You did this," as he laid on top of my back, his weight like a boulder, while he pulled down my pants and undid his own. I could hardly breathe because he was pushing me so deep into the mattress. I flailed, scratched, punched backwards, strained against his bulk, but to say it was useless doesn't quite fit. I would say it was hopeless. There was no overpowering him.

And there, in that home I'd partly grown up in for the past four years, mere feet away from his brother, his sister-in-law, and his niece, he raped me.

I'm sure it only lasted minutes. But the destruction of innocence feels like a brutally slow process while it's happening. I didn't know it was possible to feel so numb, yet battered and broken—physically and mentally—at the same time.

When he was done, he yanked me off of the bed, sending a fresh wave of pain throughout my entire lower body.

"Now see what you went and made me do? So don't tell anybody, or you gonna get and I mean get it good. Not a soul." He shoved me so hard that I stumbled out into the hall and then he closed his door again.

What just happened to me?

When Mr. Johnson shouted "Five minutes!" out of the bedroom door, I walked over to my backpack and picked it up. I didn't dare sit down.

Even walking was a grueling effort. So I opted to stand by the front door and wait for Ruby and Mr. Johnson. I made it to school that day. Survived the entire school day. I'm not sure if I spoke to anyone. I know I didn't learn anything. I spent the whole time trying to figure out what exactly I had done wrong. I'd been watching television, something I did all the time. I'd been waiting to go to school, something else I did on a regular basis. I'd done everything he asked me to by going with him into his room and sitting down on the bed. At what point had I done something wrong? Especially something that deserved molestation?

Even though I must have been walking around like a zombie, I don't remember anyone questioning me. Not Mr. Johnson or Ruby, my classmates or teachers, even my own mother when she came to pick me up. Even though Joseph had told me not to tell, I wondered if he had told Mama. If I'd done something wrong, wouldn't he have to tell on me? That's what most adults did. But what he'd done was wrong. I knew it wasn't supposed to have happened, so why did it? It was too much for my young mind to make sense of. So as I gently sat myself down in the passenger seat of the car, I waited for Mama to ask me what was wrong with me. She—and everyone else, in my mind—should've realized I was acting strange, that my shirt was oddly stretched out in the front, that I wasn't laughing and joking and smiling like I normally was, that I was walking funny, that I was struggling to make eye contact with people. But it was like no one cared, or even noticed. My mother didn't say a word out of the ordinary. And I kept it inside because I still wasn't positive that this horrible thing wasn't somehow my fault, just like Joseph said. So I held it. My first real secret from my mother. And I would carry it with me for more than a decade to come.

3

THOUGH I DIDN'T realize it immediately after the rape, I started to notice that I had developed a fear of being around men at about thirteen years old. Before, I would happily go with my mother's brothers or Dalton and his friends to a ballgame or a movie. Now, I would retreat to my room whenever they came over. I would flinch when they tried to pat me on the back, hesitate when they called me over, and felt nervous if they happened to be walking behind me. Being raised by my grandmother, spending mostly time with my mother and my father's daughters, I was surrounded by females on a day-to-day basis. So being around women was where I felt most comfortable anyway. But I'd never actively avoided men before. Now I found myself doing so. I didn't want them to do what Joseph had done.

That feeling of being unseen was still with me. It seemed like I didn't belong anywhere. If I spent too much time with my female friends or my Granny, Dalton and other men in my life would say I needed to spend more time around men. When I spent more time around men, I spent the entire experience shaking like a leaf, worried that I'd be victimized again by someone that I knew and trusted. Even though I got to spend time with Granny, not being able to live with her permanently meant I didn't really belong there. But in Orlando, Joseph was still part of our lives, so it wasn't comfortable in my own home either much of the time. I watched Patrick have his father teaching and nurturing him every day, while I couldn't get the same thing from my own dad. I felt like I needed him more than ever, but was physically and emotionally farther away from him than I'd ever been. I might get a call on a holiday or a birthday, but that was about it. Not even those cringe-worthy talks at the front of Granny's house.

Feeling so disconnected like this pushed me to do what I could to get that sense of belongingness and acceptance that I hadn't felt since before the assault. I was an honor roll student and that got me some attention, but it wasn't enough. I tried joining the football team, and even got good at it. That helped a bit, too. Still, I kept looking. There was a group of kids at school who regularly were absent. They were intentionally skipping school and when I was invited to join in, I didn't pass up the opportunity. We didn't do anything too crazy, mostly just hung out at each other's houses, but it was the most belongingness I'd felt out of everything I'd tried so far. This small bunch of kids had accepted me into their group and we were sharing a special experience with one another. I even pretended that I'd had sex with girls like some of the other boys (claimed to) had done. I'd do anything just to feel like I fit in somewhere. Even though I was enjoying feeling connected to these other kids, I was also terrified of Mama finding out.

But even skipping school and lying about sex didn't make my anxiety and feelings of loneliness and shame go away completely. They were just distractions from a growing problem. By the time I was fifteen, I was regularly experiencing depressive symptoms and having thoughts of killing myself. I didn't really belong anywhere, so why be here at all? What was the point? At least, if I died, the pain, confusion, and resentment I felt at being victimized would stop.

But, underneath it all, I think I really just wanted somebody to acknowledge what had happened to me. For someone to reach out, to show that they cared. The only time anyone came close to doing this was when I would do something or say something deemed to be "effeminate." At that point, people could talk all day about something being off about me. Yet not a single person thought to ask if someone had hurt me. If something had happened to me. And I didn't have the skills or the strength to fight against my shame and embarrassment and bring it up myself. So I acted out instead.

4

HAD THINGS CONTINUED along this path, I probably would have ended up committing suicide. By the sheer grace of God, another boy on the football team with me, Lance, asked me if I wanted to come to the youth Bible study at his church. Internally, I rolled my eyes. The last thing I wanted to do was sit in some dusty church with a bunch of elderly people nodding while a preacher droned on about Hell, Jesus, and sins. When I was a kid, that was all I knew and I was fine with it. But now, I struggled to get through church when Mama took me, so I definitely didn't want extra time there. I had the "no" ready, but then he jumped into describing their Bible study. It sounded more like a party to me. And he seemed to genuinely look like he enjoyed it because he kept smiling and laughing as he talked. I figured it was worth a shot. It couldn't be any worse than the churches I'd been to with Mama and Granny. And if his description was accurate, it might even be fun. Short of the time we spent waiting for everyone to get into the room, everything about the event was just like Lance described it. The Bible study itself was filled with testimonies from people my age, so a lot of the content was more relevant to what I was going through: girls, thinking about college, doing chores, becoming a responsible adult, learning how to drive, and so on. Now they had my attention! But then there were breaks where there was singing and dancing. Not the solemn hymns they would sometimes drone through at the AME in Allendale, or even Mama's church in Orlando, but songs with rhythm and melody that sounded like something I might hear on the radio. I could hardly believe it! Before I knew it, there was a warmth that I can only attribute to God Himself, that flowed all throughout my body. I felt like I was being cradled in God's hands, like a baby. I was filled with a love and peace like I hadn't known in years. And even though I hadn't cried the day I was raped, or that night, or at any point after that, I did it then. In a room filled with boys I didn't know and had never met, besides Lance, I wept. And with each tear, a little more resentment, a little more loneliness, a little more bitterness seeped out of my soul. In that moment, my desire to die vanished and I felt safe and loved. I couldn't think of anything else to do at that moment but pray. As the Bible study went on, and I heard the praise of, and teaching about, Christ and God, I wondered if this could be a place where I belonged. Even though these were technically strangers, didn't our love of God make us all family, in a way? Even being clear-minded and good-spirited enough to think this way was evidence of how much of the shame and anxiety that I normally carried around with me had disappeared. I knew at that moment that God was covering and healing me, just like he had when I was in a coma as a little boy. My spirit felt massive relief that day. At the end of the service, there was an altar call. I had heard of them before, but never actually experienced one myself. I didn't hesitate to go to the altar and surrender my life to God. That day, because of the messenger, Lance, that God had sent my way, my life was saved. Now it was time for me to start living it in a God-centered way.

5

AT THE AGE of twenty-one, I was experiencing a major identity crisis. I was constantly asking myself why I, of all the people in the world, had to be the one who got abused. And why, in the face of so many people remarking on my "feminine" ways, was I the one having to fight for my manhood? Even though Dalton did a wonderful job as a role model and father figure in my life, he wasn't my biological father. So that piece of my life was still missing. I wanted that validation from my own father.

By not getting it, since my father was still mostly a voice on a phone line, I felt frustrated when I found myself becoming attracted to men. Like the abuse I suffered, it was something that I didn't want, but that was forced upon me anyway. There was still a little boy inside of the man I had become. And that little boy needed healing and support. But, once again, a messenger of God was sent to give me what I needed.

While I was helping one of the pastors at Lance's church—now my church home as well—with some skits we were preparing for Sunday service the next day, she joked "You gonna help me preach tomorrow." I laughed, she smiled. I knew she was kidding and didn't think much more about it, though the mere inkling that I would ever get up and speak in front of the entire congregation was horrifying! Even doing something scripted and rehearsed was a big step for me, so the idea of having to think of what to say and how to say it and then get the words out of my mouth all on a whim was just too far outside my comfort zone to even consider.

The next day, we did the skit as scheduled and everything went off without a hitch. I was still a bit nervous, but since it all worked out well, I felt a lot better when the performance was over. My mother had come from her church to see me in my role and I smiled and waved as I prepared to get off of the stage. But just as I was reaching the top of the few steps at the edge of the platform, the pastor handed me the mic, turned me around, and said "Be free!"

The surprise and fear hit me all at once. Though there may have been a hundred or so people present, there might as well have been a thousand or even a million. How could she force me to speak in front of all these people? And about what?

But, much like when I had gone to this church for the first time at sixteen, that same warmth and peace spread over me. Suddenly I knew exactly what I needed to say. Really, what I had been wanting to say to someone—anyone—for over ten years.

"I...I've been struggling. With depression. And even suicidal thoughts. And all because, when I was ten years old..." it took everything in me not to make eye contact with my mother just then. I knew that if I did, I would break down before I could get the words out. So I just looked at the crucifix hanging above the sanctuary doors.

"...a close family friend took me into his room and molested me."

The entire room seemed to gasp at the

same time. Some people started to shout out to God to help and heal me. Others just stared at me, stunned. My mother immediately broke down crying and I fought back tears as I let the rest of my burdens down. I told them all about skipping school and acting out. About being ridiculed by loved ones because of the way I talked, walked, and dressed. About feeling like there was no place for me in this world until I walked through these very doors five years beforehand.

When I was done speaking, I felt a huge weight lifted off of me. That sense of suffocation and screaming without being heard was gone. I felt like I could fully breathe now. Until that moment, I hadn't realized just how powerful confession can be and how much healing and empowerment it can provide. Now that the trauma had been brought to light, I could start to work on addressing it. It's hard to fix a problem no one talks about. Even though I expected and wanted my mother to come to me and ask what was wrong, I'd finally been pushed into asking and answering that question for myself instead. I never had to wait for someone to ask me for my story. I always could have told it.

After church, I had a long conversation

with Mama about what I had experienced. This was one of the most difficult talks I'd ever had with anyone. I didn't consider how painful it would be to relive that time in Joseph's room and to reveal to Mama who had done this to me. As I told her, she couldn't hold back her tears. And she told me something that both crushed and angered me. She'd been sexually abused, too. And so had my grandmother.

I was reeling. Not only did I see that it wasn't just me who this had happened to, but it seemed like some kind of generational curse. I wondered why, if she'd been through the same thing, and her mother had, she didn't check on me? Ask questions? I knew this cycle had to stop.

I also learned that childhood molestation affects everyone differently. In some cases, people can become promiscuous due to the early exposure to sexual acts. Others become fearful and closed off from other people, never wanting to even be touched again, regardless of the gender of that person. Still others experience identity confusion, like myself, not knowing which gender they most connect with.

This breakthrough, once and for all, gave me the courage to stand in my truth and understand that what happened to me was not my fault. This gave me the strength to embrace my God-given manhood and embody everything about being a man that I appreciate. The strength, courage, resilience, wisdom, and—most of all— love. I knew I had the power to love myself and to love others. From that point on at church, my relationships with the members were still as open and loving as always. The biggest difference was that some of the people in the congregation who had experienced similar trauma shared it with me. Though my mother and grandmother never went on to seek professional help for their abuses, I did. I knew I deserved to get help to heal. What happened to me wasn't fair and the very least I could do was get the assistance I needed.

Two years later, when I was twenty-three, I got one of my periodic calls from my father while I was at work. He asked me about my day and how long my shift was and said to call him when I got home. I thought this was a little strange, but I figured he just had more to talk about and didn't want me to be at work on my phone. So, I planned to do as instructed and call him back as soon as I got home.

But when I pulled into my apartment

complex that night, there he was, standing in the parking lot. I was shocked, but glad to see him. He told me he was hoping to spend the weekend in town and wanted to spend some time with me if I had any free. This was a huge development. Most of the time he came down, it was for a holiday and we would spend time all together as a family. But this was the first time he said he wanted to spend time with me only.

Over the years of sporadic calls from him, I had resigned myself to the fact that he would never do more for me than that. Whether he refused to, or couldn't, the result was the same. So I convinced myself to let go of wanting that closeness and validation from him. But during this "porch" conversation in the parking lot, he said "You're more man that I could have ever raised. I look up to you."

And I once again bawled like a child. Something that I had been waiting over two decades to get from my father was finally being delivered to me by God. I was grateful, surprised, and relieved. We hugged and I told him to come stay with me the entire time he was in town. That time we spent together was true, quality time between father and son. Actually saying the words, "I resented you for not being there," took another load off of my spirit. I still didn't tell him about being raped for the sake of taking things one hurdle at a time. But, at that time, the little boy that had been trapped inside this grown man's body of mine could finally be set free. From this point forward, my father and I would have a closer, more authentic relationship.

6

ABOUT FOUR YEARS later, when I was twenty-seven, I ended up reconnecting with a former middle school classmate. We started dating and it wasn't long before we fell in love. We were married in February of 2014. That was one of the happiest days of my life. Even though they got to see me walk down the aisle, both my mother and my grandmother passed away that year. My mother died in August, at the age of 42, from cervical cancer. Granny died that December. Two pillars of my life were gone in less than a year. It was devastating.

But to start the very next year after that

one, my son was born. From the second I looked at him, I made it my mission to ensure he would never go through the hurt that I did as a child. He would have his father actively in his life. He would grow up in a household with two parents who were married and loved each other. He would have parents who took care of him and encouraged him to speak on whatever was going on with him. Every chance I get, I affirm and validate my son as a young man, and I allow him to experience what real, healthy love should feel like.

Due to my trauma, my wife and I are very guarded with where our children can go, especially regarding overnight stays with friends or family members. I encourage you to remember that, just because someone is a blood-relative doesn't mean that their intentions are pure or that they can be trusted with your child. I strongly believe that "it takes a village to raise a child." But I hope you'll actively pay attention to and manage who is part of that village. So, today, I'm married, have a son and a daughter, am able to be an active father in my children's lives, and run a firm that provides after school programming for children. I am both happy and fulfilled as a father, brother, and husband, but also as a man. Having the validation of my father really helped me in my self-discovery. Many of us are searching for who we are and trying to become the person we envision ourselves to be. I learned that validation from your parents, and a mother or father affirming who you are, is more powerful than you know. Words shape and mold our lives and affirm our character. Since human beings learn the most in the first three years of life, this is a critical time to use our words and behavior to shape our children. Whatever trauma you have experienced as a child does not have to dictate the outcome of your life. You have the power to make a definitive decision to not allow the pain someone else causes you to shape your existence. I learned the hard way that it's okay to not be okay. Admitting that you need help and seeking that help is a huge milestone in your healing journey. Whether it is a counselor, psychologist, or spiritual leader, seek professional help so you can be guided in the right direction. Despite the horrific words my abuser spoke to me—"It's your fault."—I have been able to successfully overcome depression and turn that tragedy into triumph. Whatever you may have gone through in life up to this point, I hope my story can serve as a testament that you can overcome it. You don't have to be a product of your pain. You don't have to remain the scared child that had their innocence taken away. Start to heal from your past trauma through open communication, addressing issues directly instead of sweeping them under the rug, and trusting in the will and power of God.

About the Author

As a charismatic, innovative, and vision-driven humanitarian, Donovan Gardner bravely allows an unambiguous view into his personal trauma to give a voice to the wounds of others.

As the first-time author of the eagerly awaited *The Boy Inside the Man*, a memoir that navigates his intrepid journey through childhood victimization, Donovan champions the reality that we don't have to be a product of our pain. Born in Allendale, South Carolina, and raised in a single-parent home, the door to Donovan's trauma was opened when he was molested by a family friend. Donovan's memoir walks us through his journey of healing and reinvention, as his growth transformed him into the high-powered, optimistic, visionary who now dedicates his life to the empowerment of others. Donovan is an author, speaker, coach, entrepreneur, and youth advocate. In the fulfillment of these roles, he applies the motto "Empowered today, equipped tomorrow." Donovan's innovative, holistic approach to pedagogy influences individuals, unifies teams, and invigorates leaders by building a bridge between where they are now and where they want to be. Donovan has dedicated his career to youth advancement, which is reflected in his recent charter of a Grassroots educational organization in 2019 which earned a contract with one of the largest school districts in the nation in 2020.

Driven by his passion for philanthropy and community involvement, Donovan's humanitarian efforts are reflected in his dedication to many nonprofit organizations. Donovan has played a critical role in organizing food and toy drives for organizations such as Second Harvest Food Bank, Toys for Tots, and The Just Because Foundation. His philanthropic pursuits include the awarding of hundreds of scholarships for after-school care to historically underserved students. Above all of his numerous passions, Donovan is most dedicated to his family. The reinforcement behind Donovan's drive, purpose, and distinction is his wife and two children.